D1570576

CHEF

CAREERS WITH EARNING POTENTIAL

CAR MECHANIC

CHEF

COSMETOLOGIST

DOG GROOMER

MASSAGE THERAPIST

FARMER

THE ARTS

PRESENTING
YOURSELF

CAREERS WITH EARNING POTENTIAL

CHEF
A CULINARY ARTIST

Christie Marlowe and Andrew Morkes

MASON CREST
PHILADELPHIA
MIAMI

Mason Crest
450 Parkway Drive, Suite D
Broomall, Pennsylvania 19008
(866) MCP-BOOK (toll-free)
www.masoncrest.com

First printing
9 8 7 6 5 4 3 2 1

ISBN (hardback) 978-1-4222-4323-7
ISBN (series) 978-1-4222-4319-0
ISBN (ebook) 978-1-4222-7487-3

Cataloging in Publication Data on file with the publisher.

NATIONAL
HIGHLIGHTS

Developed and Produced by National Highlights, Inc.
Editor: Andrew Gance
Interior and cover design: Jana Rade, impact studios
Interior layout: Tara Raymo, CreativelyTara
Production: Michelle Luke
Proofreader: Abby Jaworski

QR CODES AND LINKS TO THIRD-PARTY CONTENT

KEY ICONS TO LOOK FOR:

 WORDS TO UNDERSTAND: These words with their easy-to-understand definitions will increase the reader's understanding of the text while building vocabulary skills.

 SIDEBARS: This boxed material within the main text allows readers to build knowledge, gain insights, explore possibilities, and broaden their perspectives by weaving together additional information to provide realistic and holistic perspectives.

 EDUCATIONAL VIDEOS: Readers can view videos by scanning our QR codes, providing them with additional educational content to supplement the text. Examples include news coverage, moments in history, speeches, iconic sports moments, and much more!

 TEXT-DEPENDENT QUESTIONS: These questions send the reader back to the text for more careful attention to the evidence presented there.

 RESEARCH PROJECTS: Readers are pointed toward areas of further inquiry connected to each chapter. Suggestions are provided for projects that encourage deeper research and analysis.

 SERIES GLOSSARY OF KEY TERMS: This back-of-the-book glossary contains terminology used throughout this series. Words found here increase the reader's ability to read and comprehend higher-level books and articles in this field.

WORDS TO UNDERSTAND

catering: providing food for many people who are attending an event such as a wedding or meeting

entry-level job: one that requires only basic skills

fulfilling: something that is very satisfying and rewarding

lavish: expensive or impressive

vegan: a person who does not eat meat, poultry, fish, or any of their by-products

CHAPTER 1

FOOD AND SOCIETY

THE MAGIC OF FOOD

We need food to live. It provides energy and nutrition as we go about our daily lives, but food is much more than that. In fact, food is at the heart of many important life events. It helps people to connect and celebrate. For example, we eat lavish dinners at fancy restaurants to celebrate birthdays, weddings, religious festivals, anniversaries, and many other life events. Families go to casual restaurants, or perhaps even nice ones, to celebrate good grades, birthdays, a big win in a junior-league baseball game, and for tons of other reasons. And tasty, celebratory meals are even cooked at home by your mom or dad, or perhaps a personal chef.

What's also amazing about food is that it is never boring because of the sheer variety of sources throughout the world. The Food and Agriculture Organization of the United Nations estimates that there are 250,000 to 300,000 species of edible plants around the world. That's a lot of different ingredients for recipes!

Many people head to restaurants to celebrate important life events (birthdays, anniversaries, etc.), or simply to have some fun with friends.

TURNING YOUR LOVE OF FOOD INTO A CAREER

It's clear that we love to eat, but many people also love working in the food industry. Did you know that there are dozens of career opportunities in this field? For example, *food critics and writers* review the dishes at restaurants and write about culinary trends, popular new dishes, and almost any other chow-related topic in which they're interested. *Food marketing* workers are employed by production companies. They design marketing campaigns that tell the public about new food products. *Dietitians* and *nutritionists* are experts in the helpful qualities of food and give advice to people to help them lead a healthy lifestyle or reach a specific health-related goal. And then, of course, there are *chefs*, *cooks*, and *food preparation workers*—the professionals who actually make what we eat.

Choosing a career may seem daunting at first. But keep in mind that when young people imagine their futures, they see different things. Some imagine themselves wearing a business suit, in charge of a company. Others see themselves learning in a college classroom. Still others may picture themselves running down the field as a member of a professional sports team, taking someone's temperature in a doctor's office, or cooking in a restaurant. As a young person, you don't have to know exactly what you want to do after high school. It's ok to explore lots of ideas. And it's ok to change your mind along the way.

Some people, though, seem to know what they want to do from an early age. For example, Aarón Sánchez, co-star of the Food Network series *Chopped*

One of the most exciting careers in the food industry is that of chef.

CHEF VS. COOK

What's the difference between a chef and a cook? A couple things. If you're cooking at home for family, friends, and yourself, you're a cook. Chefs get paid to cook food. Some cooks work in restaurants too, and they do get paid as well. Cooks who work in casual-style restaurants and diners generally don't have to be too creative about their cooking, though. They follow recipes, flip hamburgers, make scrambled eggs, and fry French fries. Chefs usually have more knowledge and more training. Chefs come up with menus, don't need recipes to create delicious meals, and understand the science behind the dishes they're making. In this book, we'll talk a lot about chefs but also discuss cooks and other culinary professionals.

and *Heat Seekers*, knew he wanted to be a chef from a young age. When he was twelve or thirteen, he began working in the kitchen of his mother's restaurant after school. (His mother, Zarela Martinez, is a famous chef in her own right.) "It just became something I really enjoyed, and it was one of the few things I was good at," Aarón explained in an interview found on the Institute of Culinary Education's website. "I was a very undisciplined child, and the kitchen was good because it provided structure, mentoring, and discipline—something every young person needs."

Other people are a little less sure. Take Trine Hahnemann, a famous chef and food writer in Denmark. "I never thought it was going to be my career, [but] it was always my passion [an intense love for an activity] to cook," she recalls in an interview found at reluctantgourmet.com. "I collected cookbooks and cooked for my family and friends and for parties." Trine discovered she could turn her passion to cook into a career a little later in life, even though when she was younger, she never imagined she would become a chef.

Maybe like Aarón and Trine, you also love to cook. Even if you've never thought about becoming a chef, a love of cooking just might be the first step to a rewarding culinary career! However, you'll need a lot more than just a passion for preparing food in order to become a successful chef.

COOKING UP SUCCESS

Chefs are key members of a restaurant's staff. They prepare imaginative and tasty dishes for customers who are enjoying a night out. Chefs are different from cooks at home because they've had training and lots of practice—and they get paid for making food.

You may not have seen many chefs in your life because they usually work behind the scenes. You'll find them in the kitchens of many restaurants or at

Cooks make most of the food we eat on a regular basis—hamburgers and fries, pancakes and omelets, and chicken noodle soup and chili.

Chefs are highly trained professionals who turn the preparation of food into an art form.

catering companies. Chefs also work in more unusual places, like on cruise ships, at amusement parks, in food trucks, and in private homes (as personal chefs). You may have seen a celebrity chef on TV or in magazines or online. They are famous people who have made names for themselves through cooking. Maybe your family has a cookbook written by one. Celebrity chefs are a hit these days. Lots of people know who Emeril Lagasse and Rachael Ray

Learn what it takes to become a chef in a top-rated restaurant.

FACTS ABOUT THE U.S. RESTAURANT INDUSTRY

- There are more than one million restaurants.
- Nine out of ten restaurants have fewer than fifty employees.
- Approximately 14.7 million people work in the industry.
- Ninety percent of restaurant managers started out in **entry-level jobs**.
- Eighty percent of restaurant owners began their careers in entry-level positions.

Source: National Restaurant Association

are, whether from cooking shows on TV or the internet, cookbooks, or television commercials. Some chefs become famous for being experts in a certain field. For example, Chloe Coscarelli and Roberto Martin are well-known vegan chefs.

Successful chefs can become celebrities with a lot of hard work and some luck. Of course, most chefs don't end up with so much fame, but their jobs are fulfilling and provide a sense of satisfaction. While being a chef isn't right for everyone, it can be a great choice for many people who already love to cook.

Chefs don't generally need to go to a traditional (regular) four-year college to start working or to be successful. Being a chef is one of the many career choices for young people who may find that college is not right for them.

COLLEGE OR NOT?

Thinking about college can be stressful. You need to make decisions about where to apply, what programs to consider, and how far from home you want to be. But first, you have to decide whether you even want to go to college! Most high school graduates do end up going to a two- or four-year college, but not all. In 2016, nearly seven out of every ten students in the United States who graduated from high school went on to attend college, according to the U.S. Department of Labor (USDL). The other 30 percent participated in an apprenticeship, joined the military, or went right into the workforce instead.

College can be a great way to learn new things, build your independence, and start a career. But it isn't for everyone. Some people learn better outside the classroom, and some just can't afford to go to college. A postsecondary education can be very expensive. A year of college can cost anywhere from a few thousand dollars to more than $50,000, depending on the school. Huge student loans can be a real problem for people who do go to college. Student loans provide money that students borrow to pay for their education and must pay back after graduation. The *Wall Street Journal* reports that students who graduated from college with debt (money owed to a person, company, or organization) had average debt of $37,712. This much debt takes more than ten years to pay off! Some young people just aren't willing to take that risk. They would rather work and make money than pay for college. Additionally, studies have shown that some college graduates cannot find a job that is a good match for their degree or they can only find jobs that don't require a university degree!

Whatever you decide, you should think about your decision long and hard before you make up your mind. Choosing to go to college, or skipping college and going straight to work or other training, is an important step. Gather as much information as you can find; talk to your school counselors, teachers, and other adults; and check out colleges or potential jobs so you know what you're getting yourself into.

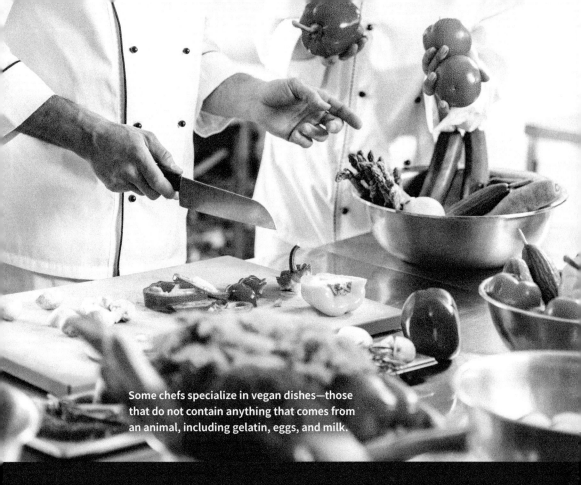

Some chefs specialize in vegan dishes—those that do not contain anything that comes from an animal, including gelatin, eggs, and milk.

RESEARCH PROJECT

Talk to chefs, food critics, dietitians, and others who work in food-related careers. Ask them what they like and dislike about their jobs. Write a short report that details your findings. Which career do you think would be the best fit for you?

TEXT-DEPENDENT QUESTIONS

1. What's the difference between a chef and a cook?
2. What are some other food-related careers?
3. Where do chefs work?

WORDS TO UNDERSTAND

camaraderie: the trust and friendship that are felt by two or more people while working together on a shared task

cuisine: a style of cooking from a certain country or region, such as Italian cuisine or Southern cuisine

full-service restaurant: one that includes table service where a waiter takes customers' orders at the table and brings the food out

parliament: a group of people that make laws; parliament is a little like the U.S. Congress

CHAPTER 2

WHAT DO CHEFS DO?

THE WORK OF CHEFS

Every chef has a different job to do. Some work as part of a team preparing meals at restaurants. Some are in charge of restaurants. Some invent and test new recipes for food companies. Others work as personal chefs. Still others work in food trucks and sell their creations all over a city. What they all have in common is cooking. Being a chef is more than just cooking, however. People are often surprised to learn chefs must also do everything from keeping track of money and supplies to hiring and training new workers. A chef is always busy, and no day is ever the same!

TYPES OF CHEFS

Not all chefs have exactly the same job. Some work in huge kitchens, and some work in tiny ones. Some chefs work mostly by themselves, while others work with several or more than a dozen other people.

The chefs with white aprons and hats that most people think about are *executive chefs*. They are in charge of a whole kitchen and make the most complicated recipes. They might direct other chefs and kitchen workers. Many celebrity chefs are famous because of their jobs as executive chefs.

Underneath executive chefs are *sous chefs*. A sous chef makes many of the recipes and knows a lot about cooking and food preparation. They are the second-in-command and can take charge if the executive chef is gone for a while. Sous chefs may eventually become executive chefs if they work long enough and have a lot of talent.

Chefs work in a variety of settings, but most are employed at traditional restaurants.

An award-winning chef provides advice to those who aspire to a career in the culinary arts.

Chefs work in all sorts of places. Most work in restaurants. According to the U.S. Department of Labor (USDL), 53 percent of chefs work in full-service restaurants. Another 10 percent work in traveler accommodations, which mostly means hotels and motels. The rest of the chefs in the United States work in all sorts of places, including private homes, amusement parks, and company cafeterias.

Then there are chefs who have completely unique jobs. Walter Scheib, for example, was the executive chef at the White House from 1994 to 2005. He cooked for the president and his family, for visiting leaders, and for parties of a hundred or more. "I get to do every day what most chefs get to do once or twice in their life, if they're lucky," he told *The New York Times* in 1998. No one else in the world has the exact same job!

Another interesting job is found in the fast food industry—somewhere you probably don't expect to find a chef. For example, Michael Haracz is the manager of culinary innovation at McDonald's. He helps to research and develop new dishes for the McDonald's menu. This type of culinary professional is known as a *research chef*. "Because we work with so many different people, on any given day, we can have ten or more chefs working on a project," Michael explains at McDonalds.com. "Members of the culinary team all come from diverse backgrounds, but are well-trained in multiple culinary disciplines, and bring new and creative ideas to the table."

MORE THAN JUST COOKING

Of course, chefs cook. Although cooking isn't their only activity, it is the reason why most chefs chose the profession. A big part of their time is spent actually preparing food for a restaurant or other food business.

They learn how to prepare all sorts of recipes, like soups, breads, and meat dishes. A good chef generally doesn't

DOZENS OF CHEFS!

Depending on the restaurant, there may be one chef in the kitchen, or dozens. In larger kitchens, every chef has their own title. Here are some of them:

- **Executive chef:** in charge of the entire kitchen
- **Sous chef:** second-in-command, literally "under chef"
- **Sauté chef:** cooks all sautéed foods and their sauces
- **Fish chef:** cooks all fish dishes
- **Grill chef:** cooks all grilled foods
- **Vegetable chef:** cooks appetizers, vegetable side dishes, and vegetable main dishes
- **Pantry chef:** prepares cold foods like salads and cold appetizers
- **Pastry chef:** makes baked goods

A baker removes freshly cooked bread from an oven.

need a recipe. They work from memory and know the ingredients, amounts of ingredients, and the directions. They also know a lot of cooking techniques. Most can whip up a soufflé (a baked egg-based dish) or make perfect bread without any problem.

Most chefs specialize in some sort of cooking style. In the past, the most well-known and well-paid cooked French food, but today, you'll find talented chefs cooking gourmet burgers, vegetarian food, and Asian cuisine. The best chefs use really good ingredients and know how to come up with combinations of flavors that wow customers.

Jason Fox, who owns a restaurant in San Francisco, knows what it's like to cook in the kitchen. He explains that he and his fellow chefs ask themselves, "Where does this come from? How can we tweak this texture? How can we play with flavor? How can we take something familiar and maybe change it a little bit so it's still comforting but surprising?" The process can be long, but chefs

A cherry soufflé.

enjoy it because they love cooking so much. Jason says, "We just talk about stuff all the time. It has to be delicious, at least according to us, first. And then we like just when there's a surprise to it, a twist. I think it seems more interesting. For us, we're just trying to do the path of it's delicious, but there's [a] surprise, there's a little fun to it." Chefs are always trying to come up with new and exciting recipes.

What you might not realize is chefs spend a lot of time doing things other than cooking. They sit at a desk, planning out meals and organizing the restaurant. Executive chefs are the most likely to spend a lot of time planning because they're in charge of the kitchen. Sometimes executive chefs also own the restaurant where they cook and have to keep track of what is going on in the whole business, not just the kitchen.

Here are just some of the things a chef might need to do to plan for the meals ahead:

- **Create new recipes and figure out how to make them in the restaurant.** Diners don't like to eat the same things forever, so chefs are often in charge of figuring out how to change the menu to keep people coming back for more. They collect ideas, try new ingredients, and play with recipes to get them just right. Many chefs think this is one of the best parts of their job.

KITCHEN DANGERS

The kitchen can be a dangerous place! Chefs and head cooks have one of the highest rates of injuries and illnesses of all careers, according to the USDL. Chefs have to be careful of knives, which they use every day. They must also take care around stoves, ovens, and other pieces of kitchen equipment. With training, chefs learn how to use all of these things properly and safely. Chefs work fast, and they stand for long hours.

High heat and the occasional controlled burst of flames during the food preparation process are just a few of the dangers chefs encounter as part of their jobs.

Over time, the heat, standing, and quick work can cause health issues such as exhaustion, back problems, or sore knees and ankles. Finally, chefs have to make sure the food itself is safe. They can't let meat sit out on the counter for hours, or let food get moldy in the fridge. Food that hasn't been prepared or cooked right can make customers sick. If a restaurant develops a reputation for making people sick, it won't be in business long.

- **Order food.** Chefs must get the ingredients for the recipes they make and serve. They can't run out of food in the middle of dinner, and they can't order too much or it will all go bad before it can be cooked. Chefs figure out where the best places are to order ingredients, and how and when they will be delivered. Some chefs may even travel to local farms and growing facilities to choose the best produce and other foodstuffs for their kitchen.

- **Figure out budgets.** Buying ingredients takes money, and some chefs are in charge of paying for ingredients, paying kitchen workers, and ordering kitchen equipment. If a chef owns the restaurant, they have to also keep track of the money spent on decorations, paying waiters, and heating and cooling the building. They also have to set menu prices in order to make a profit.
- **Keep track of kitchen equipment.** Chefs need to know exactly what's going on in the kitchen. If a piece of equipment breaks—like a stove or mixer—the chef needs to know right away and have a plan to replace or fix it.
- **Know and follow food safety rules.** The kitchen a chef works in must follow food safety laws. Food safety laws protect diners from getting sick from the food they're eating. If the chef doesn't know the laws, or doesn't make sure the kitchen is following them, people could get sick or the facility could lose its license (official permission given by the government to operate a business) to serve food.
- **Manage the kitchen staff.** Chefs are often in charge of other people. In large kitchens, many chefs might be working at once. Kitchens also have food preparation workers and dishwashers, and waiters may be in and out. A chef may have to hire these people, train new workers, and make sure everyone is doing their job correctly.

DAILY LIFE FOR COOKS

Day to day, the work of a chef can be really hard. They work long hours and often at unusual times. They work in the very early mornings, late at night, on

Chefs need to learn how to work in close quarters.

weekends, and on holidays. They might work for twelve or more hours at a time. Think about all the times you might go to a restaurant—that's when chefs have to work. Nights or weekends off are rare.

The kitchen can be a stressful and busy place. Multiple chefs are preparing food nonstop. Workers are washing dishes, chopping onions, and whisking plates away to serve to diners. Stoves and ovens are on, making it hot and stuffy. Kitchens are full of smells—some tasty and some not so great. Raw fish have to be prepared, no matter how smelly they might be!

Kitchen staff may not always get along. With so many people trying to do so many different jobs jammed into a small space, it's no surprise that kitchen workers can lose their cool sometimes.

But as chef Trine Hahnemann says, "I love the atmosphere in the kitchen, I love the business, the timing, and the teamwork! I do not believe you have to shout or go crazy to run a smooth kitchen with service on time." While all that is going on in a kitchen might overwhelm some people, Trine finds it to be one of the best parts of her job.

Jason also finds the kitchen to be a wonderful place to work. In an interview, he said his favorite part about working in restaurants is "the creativity, the camaraderie. Everyone, we just talk about food every day, whether it's stuff we're doing, whether it's the three-star Michelin restaurant someone went to, or the new restaurant someone discovered. We create an environment where everybody thinks about food, everyone talks about food, and it's pretty open. It's pretty cool."

These two chefs don't mind the challenges of their jobs. In fact, the challenges are part of the reason they love their jobs so much.

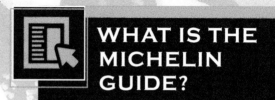

WHAT IS THE MICHELIN GUIDE?

The *Michelin Guide* ranks restaurants all over the world based on their quality. The best restaurants receive the highest rating—three stars. The guide now rates more than 30,000 establishments in over thirty territories across three continents.

GETTING THERE

So how exactly do you move from being a cook at home to being a successful chef? Young chefs almost never start out at the executive level. They have to work their way up. Jason began as a dishwasher when he was just thirteen. He

THE FIRST CELEBRITY CHEF

Julia Child is often called the first celebrity chef. Before her, chefs were just people who made food in the kitchen. However, Child became famous for teaching people how to cook French food on her TV programs and with her cookbooks. She was born in California in 1912, and spent time playing sports and working in advertising. After getting married, Child moved to Paris, where she fell in love with French food. She went to Le Cordon Bleu cooking school in Paris and eventually wrote a cookbook called *The Art of French Cooking*. The cookbook was a best seller, and was just the first of many books Child went on to write. Child also starred in several TV cooking shows. She paved the way for all the celebrity chefs we watch today. Visit https://juliachildfoundation.org to learn more about her life and work.

continued cooking and eventually had enough money and experience to open his own restaurant with a couple of partners. He says, "We always talked about the type of restaurant we'd like to have. We decided to pool our resources and found some other people who would help us out and were able to open it."

If you go to culinary school, you can expect to get a more challenging job right out of school. You've learned a lot and can step into the kitchen with some experience. If you don't go to culinary school, you may have to start closer to the bottom. Many chefs started out as dishwashers, waiters, or prep cooks. As a dishwasher, you learn a lot about the kitchen and how everything fits together. And dishwashing can be its own challenge!

Trine had a different path to becoming a professional chef. She cooked a lot when she was younger and was inspired by her grandmother. After working in the boarding school kitchen, she first decided on a different career direction as a writer. She eventually stopped going to college and focused on cooking at a café and starting her own catering business. She traveled around the world for several years, eating the foods in other countries. To Trine, that "meant a lot of dinner parties, which taught me a whole other dimension, but also living abroad gave me access to a greater variety of cooking."

When she returned from traveling, Trine decided to focus completely on cooking. Her catering business took off. She started serving food to movie and rock stars, a rare opportunity for a chef. She also caters to businesses and government organizations (like the Danish House of Parliament), appears on TV shows, and writes books. She certainly has a busy life, keeping up with all that cooking!

Professional chefs know that no matter your role in the kitchen, you'll have to work hard and learn constantly. Then, when there's an opening, your boss will know how hard you work and may promote you. You can also be on the lookout for new jobs that will take you where you want to go.

Attending culinary school is an excellent way to prepare for this career.

RESEARCH PROJECT

Talk with executive, sous, grill, fish, pastry, and other types of chefs about their work. Ask them how they broke into the field and what they like and dislike about their careers. Which occupational path seems like a good fit for your skills and interests? Write a 250-word essay that provides more information on this career.

TEXT-DEPENDENT QUESTIONS

1. In addition to cooking, what are some other duties for chefs?
2. Why can kitchens be dangerous?
3. How did Jason Fox work his way up to becoming a chef?

CHAPTER 3

TERMS OF THE TRADE

à la carte: A menu item that is priced separately from the price of a meal. For example, an à la carte item could be French fries, a baked potato, coleslaw, or grilled asparagus.

aromatics: Spices, herbs, vegetables, and sometimes meat that are cooked in oil as a base for the flavor of a dish.

bake: To use dry heat in an oven to cook.

baste: To moisten foods with seasoned liquids or fats while grilling or cooking.

blanch: To immerse a vegetable or other food product in rapidly boiling water to allow it to cook slightly.

boil: To heat a liquid until bubbles break continually on its surface.

boiling point: The temperature at which water boils. At sea level, water boils at 212° F (100° C).

broil: To cook on a grill by using strong, direct heat.

broth: Any type of seasoned liquid that has had meat cooked in it.

chop: To cut food using a knife, food processor, or cleaver.

chopping board: A wooden or plastic surface that is used when cutting food products.

cleaver: A large knife that often resembles a rectangular-bladed hatchet. Chefs and other kitchen workers use cleavers to hack through bone.

cuisine: A style of cooking from a particular country, region, or other location.

culinary arts: The arts of preparing, cooking, and presenting food.

cure: To preserve meats by salting and drying, and/or smoking, them.

dice: To cut food into small cubes of uniform shape and size.

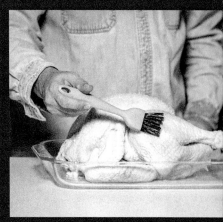

dough: A mixture of flour and liquid with other ingredients, such as shortening, sugar, salt, eggs, leavening agents, and various flavoring materials, that is used to make baked products.

dry marinade: To rub salt, pepper, herbs, or spices into meat, poultry, or seafood to enhance its flavor.

fillet: A piece of fish or meat in which there are no bones.

food processor: An appliance that is used for chopping, mixing, or pureeing foods.

fry: To cook food in hot cooking oil or fat.

full-service restaurant: One that includes table service where a waiter takes customers' orders at the table and brings the food out.

garnish: To decorate food that is about to be brought to a customer to improve its appearance; examples of garnish include parsley, raw vegetables, chopped chives, and lemon slices.

gourmet: A fan of good food.

grill: To cook on a grill over high heat.

grind: To process solids mechanically or by hand to reduce them into tiny particles.

herb: A plant with seeds, leaves, or flowers that is used to flavor food or for medicine or perfume; examples include thyme, rosemary, and mint.

julienne: To cut fruits, vegetables, or cheeses into thin strips.

ladle: A large, long-handled spoon with a cup-shaped bowl that is used to serve sauce, stew, and soup.

marinate: To add moisture and flavor to pieces of meat, seafood, poultry, or vegetables by soaking them in or brushing them with a liquid mixture of seasonings known as a marinade.

meat: The flesh of an animal (usually a mammal); examples include the flesh from cows, pigs, and poultry.

meat thermometer: A device that measures the temperature of meat.

menu: A list of dishes that are available at a restaurant or other food establishment.

mince: To chop food into tiny pieces.

parboil: Partially cooking food in boiling water.

pare: To cut off the skin or outer covering of a fruit or vegetable.

peel: To remove the peels from fruits or vegetables.

pickling: The process of preserving meats, fruits, and vegetables in brine.

plating: The careful process of presenting food attractively on a plate before it is delivered to a diner.

poach: To cook gently in hot liquid that is just below the boiling point.

poultry: Chickens, turkeys, geese, ducks, and other fowl that are raised for the production of meat or eggs.

puree: To mash foods by hand or with a mechanical device until they are perfectly smooth.

recipe: A list of ingredients and instructions that is used to make a culinary dish.

roast: To cook poultry or meat uncovered using dry heat in an oven.

rolling pin: A cylindrical kitchen utensil that is rolled over pastry or dough to shape or flatten it.

sauce: A liquid or semiliquid food that is used to make other foods look, taste, and smell better.

sauté: To cook and/or brown food in a small amount of hot fat.

scald: To bring to a temperature that is just below the boiling point.

seafood: Any fish or shellfish that comes from freshwater or saltwater.

sear: To brown very quickly by using intense heat; this is done to increase flavor and improve the appearance of a food product.

seasonings: Spices and herbs that are used to increase the flavor of food.

simmer: To cook slowly in a liquid over low heat at a temperature of approximately 180° F (82.2° C).

soufflé: A baked egg-based dish.

spatula: A kitchen utensil with a broad, flat surface that is used for mixing and spreading things.

spice: A cooking ingredient that is used to add flavor to a recipe. Spices come from the roots, bark, or seeds of a plant; examples include cinnamon, paprika, and coriander.

steaming: The process of cooking food by using vapor from boiling water.

stock: In the culinary industry, a liquid that is used as an ingredient in sauces, gravies, braises, stews, and soups. It is made by simmering a combination of animal bones (which often contain some scraps of meat), mirepoix (a mixture of carrots, celery, and onions), and aromatics in water.

tongs: A kitchen utensil that is used to grab, turn, and move food as it is being cooked or baked.

vegan: A person who does not eat meat, poultry, fish, or any of their by-products.

whip: To rapidly beat heavy cream or egg whites to introduce air and produce expansion.

whisk: A kitchen utensil that is used to blend ingredients or to incorporate air into a food mixture.

academic: having to do with learning at a college or university

aspiring: trying to reach a goal

registered apprenticeship: a program that meets standards of fairness, safety, and training established by the U.S. government or local governments

upscale: very fancy; in the culinary industry, a restaurant with high-quality ingredients and service—and often high prices

CHAPTER 4

PREPARING FOR THE FIELD AND MAKING A LIVING

BECOMING A CHEF

Pretty much every chef started out as a young cook, experimenting in the kitchen at home. Not all chefs journeyed from their home kitchens to restaurant kitchens in the same way, though. Young people who want to become chefs have several paths they can follow: going to culinary school, participating in an apprenticeship, receiving training in the military, or teaching themselves. All these paths can lead to successful careers in the food industry (a group of businesses that sell a certain product or service) as long as you're willing to work hard and stick with your dreams.

HIGH SCHOOL

Some high schools offer career and technical education programs that allow students to receive training that gives them a head start in a particular career field such as culinary arts, public safety, personal care services, hospitality, and information technology. If your high school offers a culinary arts program, sign up to begin learning how to become a chef or cook.

If your high school doesn't have such a program, there are many regular classes that will be useful to you as a chef. For example, mathematics classes will come in handy because you'll use math to determine the correct amount of ingredients to go into a recipe, track and manage supplies, and perform other tasks. Food science courses will help you understand the biological and chemical aspects of food. Speech classes will help you develop your communication skills. Writing courses will give you good preparation should you ever decide to launch a food blog or publish a cookbook. Take business, accounting, marketing, and computer science classes if you think you want to run your own restaurant someday. Learning one or more foreign languages will come in handy because restaurants—both in the kitchen and in the dining room—can be diverse places, with people from many different countries and cultures.

DID YOU KNOW?

- Half of all adults have worked in the restaurant industry at some time in their lives.
- Thirty-three percent of Americans received their first job experience in a restaurant.
- Forty percent of those surveyed say that restaurants are an important part of their lives.

Source: National Restaurant Association

CULINARY SCHOOL

Many of the most successful and famous chefs went to culinary school. These schools range from the most famous and expensive to regular colleges that offer culinary degrees to short cooking, baking, and food preparation programs at technical schools.

If you choose to go to culinary school, you should keep a few things in mind. One big consideration is cost. Many of the more famous schools provide an excellent culinary education, but they are expensive. Other culinary schools might not be well known, but they provide a solid education in cooking and are much more affordable.

An instructor assesses the work of a culinary student.

Try to learn as much as you can about culinary schools in your area to determine which offer the best education based on the cost of tuition. Visit these schools' websites, attend open houses, talk to admissions officers (professionals who help people who are applying to college), and use social media to learn about these programs. Talk to people about the schools. Perhaps you have a friend or classmate who attended one of these institutions, or maybe you can talk to an instructor in one of your target programs.

If you enroll in culinary school, you'll take many specialized classes. Some of the courses you can choose from will teach you about sauces and soups, pastry, specific cuisines such as Italian, and buffets. Non-cooking classes may include menu design, food safety, and staff management.

GET A HEAD START WITH PROSTART

ProStart is a two-year high school program in culinary arts and food service management that reaches nearly 140,000 students in more than 1,800 high schools across fifty states, Guam, and U.S. Department of Defense Education Activity schools in Europe and the Pacific. The program, which is offered by the National Restaurant Association Educational Foundation (NRAEF), helps students gain experience in the field via classes and mentored work experience in food service operations. Students can also participate in the National ProStart Invitational, a competition in which they demonstrate their culinary skills and compete for scholarships. Those who complete the program are awarded an industry-recognized certificate—the ProStart National Certificate of Achievement. Students who earn the certificate are eligible for NRAEF scholarship opportunities and course credits at select hospitality and culinary arts schools. Visit https://chooserestaurants.org/prostart to learn more about the program.

As part of your training, you'll also participate in one or more internships, which are paid or unpaid learning opportunities in which you work in a restaurant or other business to get experience. Internships can last anywhere from a few weeks to a year.

Accreditation

It's important to attend a culinary arts school that is accredited. An accredited school has met minimum standards of quality that have been set by a governing organization. If you attend an accredited school, you'll be sure to receive a top-notch education that will prepare you for a career in the culinary arts. If you attend a school that is not accredited, you may not get a great education and employers may not want to hire you.

TYPICAL CLASSES IN A CULINARY ARTS TRAINING PROGRAM

- Food Safety
- Culinary Fundamentals
- Meat Identification, Fabrication, and Utilization
- Seafood Identification and Fabrication
- Modern Banquet Cookery
- Introduction to À La Carte Cooking
- Noncommercial Food Service and High-Volume Production
- Baking and Pastry Skill Development
- Garde-Manger
- Cuisines and Cultures of the Americas
- Cuisines and Cultures of the Mediterranean
- Cuisines and Cultures of Asia
- Wine Studies
- Introduction to Hospitality and Customer Service
- Contemporary Restaurant Cooking
- Contemporary Hospitality and Service Management
- Formal Restaurant Cooking
- Formal Hospitality and Service Management

In the United States, several agencies accredit culinary arts schools and programs, including the American Culinary Federation Education Foundation Accrediting Commission (www.acfchefs.org/ACF/Education/Accreditation/ACF/Education/Accreditation) and the Accrediting Commission of Career Schools and Colleges (www.accsc.org/Directory). There are accrediting agencies in other countries too. If you don't live in the United States, check with your country's department of professional regulation for more information.

APPRENTICESHIPS

Some people train to become chefs and cooks by participating in apprenticeships. As an apprentice, you learn a particular trade. You learn via a combination of classes and hands-on experience in a kitchen. People who already know the particular trade act as your instructors, and they teach you skills along the way. Culinary apprenticeships are available throughout the world. In a registered apprenticeship training program in the United States, trainees complete 2,000 hours of on-the-job training and 144 hours of related classroom instruction. Entry requirements vary by program, but some are typical:

- Minimum age of eighteen (in Canada and some other countries, the minimum age is sixteen)
- High school education
- One year of high school algebra
- Qualifying score on an aptitude test
- Drug-free lifestyle (illegal drugs)

Culinary apprenticeships typically last from two to three years. After you finish your apprenticeship, you can open a small catering company or restaurant

A chef (center) observes two apprentices as they prepare a meal.

(or get hired by one). Graduates of apprenticeship programs are in high demand because employers know that they have received a quality education and a lot of hands-on training.

DID YOU KNOW?

Each day, more than one million meals are prepared in military kitchens, according to the U.S. Department of Defense.

MILITARY

Another option you'll have after high school is the military. Some graduates feel the military offers the right training opportunities for them. For people who want to serve their country, the military might be the right choice. Not all members of the military are sent to fight or are assigned to other countries. Many are trained in office work, as medical workers, in construction work, in the culinary arts, and more. However, if you join the military, you should be prepared for being called up to active service and possibly not being assigned to the job you want.

All five U.S. military branches (Air Force, Army, Coast Guard, Marines, and Navy), as well as many militaries in other countries, provide training for cooks and chefs. While you train, you'll receive a salary and will not have to pay any tuition, but you will have to make a service commitment of two to four years. Ask your recruiter for more information.

A U.S. Navy chef trainee measures out flour for a recipe during a bake shop class at Naval Base San Diego.

GEN Z AND MILLENNIALS AND THE FOOD SERVICE INDUSTRY

More than 70 percent of millennials (those born between 1982 and 2004) and members of Generation Z (born between 1995 and 2010) think the food service industry is a good place to get a first job, according to a survey sponsored by the NRAEF and the Center for Generational Kinetics.

SELF-TAUGHT

Another option for aspiring chefs is teaching yourself. Instead of attending culinary school, participating in an apprenticeship, or training in the military, many chefs learn through work and through experimenting with recipes at home.

Trine Hahnemann is one of those chefs. She started cooking at an early age and never stopped. "I have loved food all my life, my grandmother influenced me a lot," she says. Her first experience cooking outside the home convinced her she loved cooking. "I went to boarding school for one year when I was fifteen and cooked for one hundred people every day, and I more or less took over the kitchen on my teacher's recommendation. I loved it, but at that time it never occurred to me that this should be my profession!"

Many chefs first began developing their skills when they were teenagers.

Like many young people, Trine figured she would go to college and learn in a classroom. She explains, "I am from an academic family, and everybody goes to university. So did I." Although she ended up going to college, Trine later realized she wanted to follow a different path and become a chef. Instead of going back to school, she decided to teach herself and learn through working in kitchens.

Trine felt a little pressure to go to culinary school because many of the top chefs in the world have attended a well-known school. However, she was glad she didn't. She says, "I would not have learned so much about world cuisine and spices, and you learn so much from your mistakes as you go along, I do not think that mistakes are seen as part of the creative process in culinary school."

More and more people who want to become chefs are choosing this route because culinary school is just too expensive for them. Although learning on your own can be a long and hard process, you'll receive valuable lessons without the price tag of culinary school. As long as you're dedicated to learning new things and finding people who will teach you, you can become a great chef.

HOW MUCH CAN I MAKE?

Chefs all have at least one thing in common—they want to cook. Money isn't always their priority, as long as they get to do the work they love. However, some chefs like the glamour and often the money that comes with owning a well-rated restaurant.

No matter how famous they are, chefs generally make a good living. While not all make a lot of money, most make enough for a comfortable life. And some do make lots of money if they work in the right place.

AVERAGE PAY

Most chefs work in full-service restaurants. They earn an average of $46,100, according to the USDL.

Pay is higher at other employers. Chefs who work at amusement parks or in other recreational industries make an average of $59,810. And chefs who work at hotels and motels earn slightly less at an average of $58,170.

If you become a chef, you may not earn exactly these amounts. Some earn less and some will earn more. It all depends on how long you have been working and where you choose to work. And if you go to a culinary school first, you may start out with higher pay than someone who did not. However, you also probably had to pay for your education. Chefs who complete apprenticeships also usually earn higher salaries than those who are self-trained or who learned their skills on the job in lower-level food service positions.

SALARIES FOR CHEFS AND HEAD COOKS BY U.S. STATE

Earnings for chefs and head cooks vary by state based on demand and other factors. Here are the five states where employers pay the highest average salary and the states in which employers pay the lowest salaries.

Highest Average Salaries:
1. Hawaii: $70,480
2. New Jersey: $64,510
3. Rhode Island: $59,310
4. Massachusetts: $57,540
5. Nevada: $55,470

Lowest Average Salaries:
1. Kansas: $36,470
2. South Carolina: $37,110
3. Idaho: $38,120
4. Iowa: $38,450
5. Ohio: $38,560

Source: U.S. Department of Labor

The very first job chefs get does not generally pay high wages. For example, restaurant cooks (an entry-level position) earn salaries that range from only $18,810 to $36,440, according to the USDL. If you start out as a cook, you need to build your experience and skills before you can start to earn more. It's important not to get discouraged, though. By sticking with a fairly low-paying job, you can start to understand the culinary world. Before you know it, you'll be ready for your next job, which will have more responsibility and probably higher pay.

Chefs who have been in the business for many years might end up making more than the averages listed. After years of experience, those individuals are very skilled and can cook better than most chefs. Restaurants will pay them a

Chefs who own their restaurants have the potential to earn very high incomes.

lot to get them to cook. Chefs who have been cooking for a while may also own a restaurant, which can come with more money.

HIGH-END CHEFS

At the very top of the culinary profession are the highest paid professionals. The USDL reports that the top 10 percent of chefs make more than $78,570.

Who makes the most money? Executive chefs, who are in charge of an entire kitchen, tend to make the most. They have worked their way up. Executive chefs who work at upscale restaurants, hotels, resorts, and companies often make the most. According to PayScale.com, they can earn nearly $90,000 a year. But those same chefs probably made a lot less when they first started cooking.

Chefs make different amounts of money depending on where they live and work as well. In large cities like New York or Chicago, chefs make more money. People often come to cities to eat great food, and they're willing to pay more for a fancy meal. The chefs who work at the fanciest restaurants in large cities make more money than those who work elsewhere. For example, chefs in Washington, D.C., earn average salaries of $63,000, while those in Anchorage, Alaska, make only about $36,000.

Then there are celebrity chefs. Maybe it's your dream to someday become a famous chef with your own TV show, cookbooks, and more. While not everyone can achieve this, it's always good to have a dream! Celebrity chefs are some of the highest paid around. Besides income from restaurants, they are also paid for appearing on television shows, endorsing (recommending) kitchen products, and writing books. According to *Forbes*, Gordon Ramsay is the highest paid chef in the world. He makes $38 million a year. But keep in mind that Ramsay didn't

make most of the $38 million by sweating over a hot stove. He is a popular TV personality, author, and owner of more than twenty restaurants around the globe. Other top-earning chefs include Wolfgang Puck ($20 million), Alain Ducasse ($12 million), Nobu Matsuhisa ($10 million), and Bobby Flay ($9 million).

MONEY ISN'T EVERYTHING

Although just about everyone wants to make plenty of money, making a lot of "bread" isn't everything. You could be making tons of money but hate your job. Luckily, the people who tend to make it as chefs truly love their careers.

Gordon Ramsay is the highest paid chef in the world. He is a restaurateur, author, and television star.

Trine describes why she loves being a chef. "If I think about some of the best moments of my life, they usually involve sitting around a large table with friends and family, enjoying wonderful food…and talking of something important." Food has been an important part of her life, and she is thankful to be able to serve food to others. She loves this work, which is what keeps her going.

Money is the icing on the cake. When you love being a chef, you're more likely to make good money because you work hard at what you do. You get raises and good jobs. If you love to cook, are committed to being a chef, and work hard, you'll make a great living.

RESEARCH PROJECT

Talk to chefs who trained for the field via culinary school, apprenticeships, the military, and personal experience and/or practice. Write a report that details what you think are the best and worst aspects of each training method. Which approach is the best fit for you?

TEXT-DEPENDENT QUESTIONS

1. What are some typical classes offered by a culinary school?
2. What is involved in a culinary apprenticeship?
3. What is the average salary for a chef?

WORDS TO UNDERSTAND

character traits: the behaviors and beliefs that make up a person's personality; they may be good or bad

community college: a private or public two-year college that awards certificates and associates degrees (a two-year degree)

finances: systems of managing money

stamina: the strength to continue for a long time

CHAPTER 5

KEY SKILLS AND METHODS OF EXPLORATION

WHAT ALL CHEFS NEED

Getting a good education is important for success as a chef, but you also need a variety of skills and character traits. Here are some of the most important qualities according to the U.S. Department of Labor (USDL).

CREATIVITY

Chefs must be creative. They don't paint pictures or make music, but they do create recipes. They have to imagine what different ingredients would taste like

The best chefs love what they do and are excited to go to work every day.

with each other, and which would be the best. They can't be afraid to try unusual ingredients other chefs don't normally use and that diners aren't always familiar with. They might also have to be creative on the spot. If a food delivery to the restaurant goes wrong, or a piece of kitchen equipment breaks, the chef will have to come up with a solution right away. Creativity turns a disaster into a new recipe.

GOOD SENSE OF TASTE AND SMELL

Another important trait for chefs is a good sense of taste and smell. They create new recipes by mixing flavors together. You want to have a good handle on which tastes and smells go well together so that your meals can be the best. Some people are born with a better sense of taste and smell, but it's also something you can develop as you get older. Practicing cooking and tasting food will help.

LEADERSHIP ABILITY

Chefs must be good leaders. Executive chefs and sous chefs are often in charge of other people in the kitchen. If they are good leaders, other workers will listen to what they have to say and will follow their instructions. If a chef is a bad leader, things can easily go wrong in the kitchen and everyone else will be unhappy.

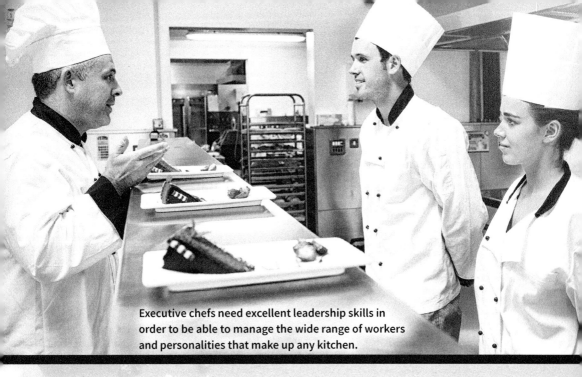

Executive chefs need excellent leadership skills in order to be able to manage the wide range of workers and personalities that make up any kitchen.

PASSION

Perhaps the most important key to becoming a chef is passion. If you do not truly want to be a chef, it will be very hard to become one. Your instructors may yell at you for doing something wrong, customers might tell you your food is tasteless, and you may work twelve or more hours a day. None of that makes any difference, though, if you are really passionate about cooking. Although you'll have some days that are better than others, you'll generally be happy and content at your job if you have a passion for what you're doing.

A love of cooking is just a start. You have to want to turn your love of cooking into a job. When you're a chef, you will be cooking all the time. You'll be sharing your creations with paying customers, not just friends and family. Being a chef is different from being a cook at home.

Becoming a chef is hard work. You need to practice cooking all the time, do homework if you're in culinary school or participating in an apprenticeship, and constantly meet new people as you search for jobs. Passion can get you through the most difficult times along the path to becoming a chef. Only the people who really want to become chefs stick with it until they land jobs.

Many people discover they love cooking when they are little. If you love to be in the kitchen and enjoy trying out new recipes, becoming a chef might be right for you. Other people realize their passion later on. Chefs have started their careers in their twenties, thirties, and even later!

BUSINESS SKILLS

Chefs who order ingredients, plan menus, or even own restaurants must be good businesspeople. A good chef will be able to understand the kitchen as a business and keep things going smoothly. You will have a hard time if you can't figure out how to manage the staff, keep track of the finances, or make a profit. Profits in a restaurant are the money left over after you pay for ingredients, employees, rent on the building, and other expenses.

Learn about the key skills for success for chefs.

OTHER SKILLS

Here are a few more key traits you'll need to be a successful chef:

- communication and decision-making skills
- physical strength, stamina, and good health
- time-management skills
- intelligence and intellectual curiosity
- willingness to continue to learn

EXPLORING CULINARY ARTS AS A STUDENT

There are many ways to explore the culinary arts. The following sections provide some suggestions.

TAKE SOME CLASSES

These days, culinary classes are everywhere. And what's great is that you can learn how to cook at any age. Cooking classes will teach you how to use kitchen tools and equipment, how to make basic recipes, the ins and outs of kitchen safety practices, and simply how to get comfortable using razor-sharp knives, working around hot stoves, and preparing and blending ingredients. The following organizations, schools, and businesses offer cooking classes:

- local park districts
- high schools
- community colleges
- culinary schools
- local restaurants
- culinary associations

Taking a cooking class is an excellent way to explore a potential career in the culinary arts.

Don't forget to check out online cooking classes. YouTube.com is a good resource, and some well-known television cooking shows offer web classes for those who want to explore the culinary arts.

DO SOME COOKING AND BAKING

Try your hand at cooking and baking. Start with easy recipes: spaghetti, blueberry pancakes, grilled cheese, or chocolate-chip cookies. Ask your mom or dad for help as you cook or bake. As you build your skills, tackle more complex recipes to build your kitchen confidence. Eventually, try to create a recipe or two from scratch. Here are some recipes for teens that will get you started:

- www.marthastewart.com/1505773/13-super-easy-meals-teens-can-make-themselves
- https://kidshealth.org/en/teens/recipes
- https://tastessence.com/easy-recipes-for-teens
- www.seventeen.com/teen-recipes

Don't forget to check out cookbooks and food-oriented books and magazines. These will help you expand your knowledge of culinary trends and different cuisines and ingredients. One useful book is *The Healthy Teen Cookbook: Around the World In 80 Fantastic Recipes* by Remmi Smith.

A group of friends learns more about cooking.

JOIN THE SCOUTS

The Girl Scouts and Boy Scouts are membership organizations for girls and boys aged roughly five to eighteen (age ranges vary by country and group). These organizations help you to become a good person and teach you many new skills. When you learn something new in scouts, you usually receive a merit badge or other type of award.

The Boy Scouts of America (www.scouting.org) is open to both boys and girls. Scouts can earn a merit badge in cooking by answering questions about food safety, nutrition, and cooking basics; developing meal plans; preparing food at home or while camping; and by fulfilling other requirements.

If you're a girl, members of the Girl Scouts of the United States of America (www.girlscouts.org) can earn a cooking merit badge.

You don't have to live in the United States to be a scout. In fact, the Boy Scouts were founded in Great Britain more than 100 years ago. Scouting

organizations in Great Britain include The Scout Association (https://scouts.org.uk) and British Boy Scouts and British Girl Scouts Association (https://bbsandbgs.org.uk). If you live in Canada, you can join Scouts Canada (www.scouts.ca). Scouts Australia (https://scouts.com.au), which was founded in 1908, has approximately 70,000 members.

PARTICIPATE IN A COMPETITION

Once you develop your cooking and baking skills, you should consider entering a cooking contest. This is an excellent way to make new friends and build your personal and professional network (a group of people you know who can help you get a job or meet other life goals). Cooking competitions are offered by park districts, local culinary organizations, schools, culinary associations, and other organizations. Check out the following competitions:

SkillsUSA

SkillsUSA is a national membership organization for middle school, high school, and college students who are preparing for careers in technical, trade, and skilled service occupations. It offers a Culinary Arts Competition in which contestants demonstrate their knowledge and skills of hot and cold food preparation and presentation through the production of a four-course menu in a full-day competition. According to SkillsUSA, "contestants are rated on organization, knife skills, cooking techniques, creative presentation, sanitation and food safety techniques, and above all, the quality and flavor of their prepared items." Competitions in Commercial Baking and Restaurant Service are also available. SkillsUSA works directly with high schools and colleges, so ask your school counselor or teacher if it is an option for you. Learn more at www.skillsusa.org.

Skills Compétences Canada

Skills Compétences Canada is a nonprofit organization that seeks to encourage Canadian youth to pursue careers in the skilled trades and technology sectors. Its National Competition allows young people to participate in more than forty skilled trade and technology competitions, including Cooking and Baking. Learn more at http://skillscompetencescanada.com/en/skills-canada-national-competition.

The winner of a National SkillsUSA culinary competition discusses his love of the culinary arts and his training to become a chef.

Students participate in a cooking contest.

Chopped Junior Competition

The Food Network's *Chopped Junior* periodically seeks contestants. Visit www.foodnetwork.com/shows/chopped-junior to learn more about the show and opportunities to compete.

JOIN A CULINARY ASSOCIATION

An association is an organization that is founded by a group of people who have the same career (engineers, chefs, etc.) or who work in the same industry specialty (restaurants, health care, etc.). Some culinary associations offer membership to teenagers. For example, the American Culinary Federation (ACF) has a Junior Culinarian membership category for high school students who are between sixteen and eighteen years of age. A membership fee is required to join the ACF, but other organizations do not charge a fee. Being a member of a culinary association provides you with a lot of different opportunities. Junior Culinarians at the ACF get access to a variety of online resources at the organization's website, such as videos and newsletters. They also are eligible to apply for scholarships, participate in competitions, and receive discounts on admission to culinary conferences. The ACF has chapters all over the United States; visit its website to find a chapter in your area.

ATTEND A SUMMER CAMP

Many young people learn more about cooking during their summer breaks. High schools, culinary schools, community groups, restaurants, and other organizations offer culinary camps and workshops. Your family and science teacher or school

SOURCES OF ADDITIONAL INFORMATION

American Culinary Federation
www.acfchefs.org

American Personal & Private Chef Association
www.personalchef.com

British Culinary Federation
www.britishculinaryfederation.co.uk

Canadian Culinary Federation
www.culinaryfederation.ca

National Restaurant Association
https://restaurant.org

New Zealand Chefs Association
www.nzchefs.org.nz/Membership.html

Research Chefs Association
www.culinology.com

Restaurants Association of Ireland
www.rai.ie

Restaurants Canada
www.restaurantscanada.org

United States Personal Chef Association
www.uspca.com

counselor can direct you to camps in your area, or you can find opportunities by doing a keyword search on the internet. Here are a few examples of well-known camps in the United States. Camps are also available in other countries.

- www.thechoppingblock.com
- www.campmasterchef.com
- https://homecookingny.com/cookingcamp
- www.blueribboncooking.com/kids-camps-parties
- http://vermontsummeracademy.org/majors/culinary-summer-camps

CONDUCT AN INFORMATION INTERVIEW WITH A CHEF

You've probably heard of a job interview, but have you heard of an information interview? In a job interview, a job seeker is asked questions by a person who is considering hiring them. An information interview is different in that you ask a chef, cook, or other culinary professional questions about their job. You can conduct this type of interview in person in the kitchen of a chef, on the telephone, via email, or online via Skype or other videoconferencing software. Here are some questions to ask during the interview:

- Can you tell me about a day in your life on the job?
- What type of equipment do you use on the job?
- What are the most important personal and professional qualities for chefs? Restaurant owners?
- What do you like best and least about your job?
- What is the future employment outlook for chefs?
- How is the field changing?

- What can I do now to prepare for the field?
- If you could go back in time, would you become a chef again?

JOB SHADOW A CHEF

In a job-shadowing experience, you watch a chef at work. You'll observe them as they slice, dice, and otherwise prepare food, create menus, manage staff, and perform other tasks. Your school counselor or a teacher can help you arrange a job-shadowing experience. You could also ask the chef at your favorite restaurant if they would like to participate. Finally, contact culinary associations for help setting up an interview. You'll find that many chefs will be happy to have you observe them on the job.

RESEARCH PROJECT

Try out three of the methods of exploration that were discussed in this chapter to learn more about cooking and a career as a chef. Write a report that details what you learned and present it to your family and consumer science class. Do you still have questions about cooking and a career as a chef? If so, use some other strategies to expand your knowledge of the culinary arts.

TEXT-DEPENDENT QUESTIONS

1. Why is passion so important for chefs?
2. What type of business skills do restaurant owners need?
3. What type of benefits are offered by a culinary association?

candidate: a person who is trying to be or is being considered for something, such as a job

consumer: a person who purchases and uses goods or services

gastronomy: the practice or art of creating good food, with a focus on gourmet cuisine

robotics: an interdisciplinary area of science and mechanical, electronic, computer, and other types of engineering that are used to create technology (robots) and operating systems to perform tasks more efficiently and less expensively than can be done by humans

CHAPTER 6

LOOKING TO THE FUTURE

GROWING OPPORTUNITIES FOR CHEFS

As long as restaurants, hotels, cruise ships, amusement parks, and cafeterias serve food, we'll need chefs—because people will always need to eat! Who else would prepare the amazing food we enjoy when making special plans to eat out?

Employment for chefs and head cooks is expected to grow by 10 percent from 2016 to 2026, according to the U.S. Department of Labor (USDL). This is faster than the average growth for all careers. The USDL says that "income growth will result in greater demand for high-quality dishes at a variety of dining venues. As a result, more restaurants and other dining places are expected to open to satisfy consumer desire for dining out." Additionally, consumer demand for healthier meals made from scratch in restaurants, in grocery stores, in cafeterias, and by catering services is creating demand for skilled chefs to oversee food preparation.

Despite the good employment outlook for chefs, there is a lot of competition for the most rewarding, high-paying jobs. What does that mean for future chefs like you? It means you'll need to get all the experience and skills you can. Chefs who already have cooking experience, who can run a business, and who are enthusiastic will have the best chance of getting a job. You might need to work at an entry-level job in a restaurant before you can become a true chef. But your job as a dishwasher or prep cook will help you get a chef job later on. Getting a good job won't always be easy—but if you believe in yourself, are willing to learn and work hard, and don't give up, your chances of success are much greater.

Chefs who are willing to consider lots of opportunities are more likely to find a job too. Not all chefs work in restaurants. Some work in cafeterias, on

Chefs will continue to be in demand because people love going to restaurants.

MOLECULAR GASTRONOMY

Molecular **gastronomy** is a subdiscipline in the culinary arts that involves food cooked using scientific principles. Chefs think about the science behind ingredients and what is happening when something is cooking. Molecular gastronomy was invented by French chef Hervé in the 1990s. Chefs who use this approach think about how ingredients are changed when they are cooked, how

Molecular gastronomy recipes.

cooking affects texture, and what smell has to do with tasting food (among other questions). Molecular gastronomy recipes include bacon-and-egg ice cream, beet foam, edible menus, and spheres of liquid tomatoes that burst on your tongue. Be prepared to be surprised—and pay a lot—if you're going out for a molecular gastronomy meal. Visit https://science.howstuffworks.com/innovation/edible-innovations/molecular-gastronomy.htm to learn more about molecular gastronomy.

cruise ships, or for food companies that are creating new products. Others work as personal chefs. Don't limit yourself to only one sort of job. Search for opportunities in all sorts of places. Get creative, and you might be surprised at what you find.

FACTORS THAT MAY SLOW GROWTH

A career in the culinary arts continues to be a popular choice for young people, but a few developments may slow growth for chefs.

If the U.S. or world economy weakens, people will have less disposable income (money that is available after living expenses—such as food, rent, etc.—are paid) to spend on meals at restaurants. They won't be able to go out to restaurants and take vacations as much, and they will eat more meals at home. If this occurs, restaurants and other dining establishments will have fewer customers. This will cause restaurant owners to reduce the work hours or even lay off some chefs and cooks. One thing to remember: A weak economy usually improves at some point, which suggests that job opportunities will increase for chefs.

Another factor that may slow growth is an oversupply of chefs and cooks. An oversupply simply means that there are more chefs and cooks than there are jobs. Oversupply happens when too many people learn about a field and decide to enter it. Every career field goes through cycles of oversupply and undersupply. One way to make yourself a more attractive job **candidate** is to

Learn how robots may change the future of cooking.

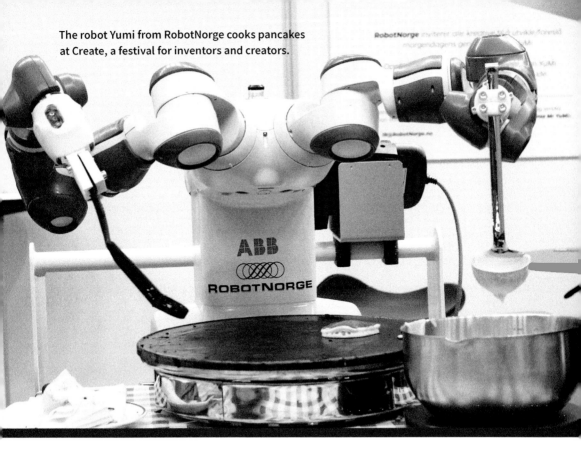

The robot Yumi from RobotNorge cooks pancakes at Create, a festival for inventors and creators.

build your skill set so that you can work in a variety of food service settings. When there is an oversupply of chefs and cooks in one area, you may have to relocate (move) to other areas where more jobs are available.

Finally, the introduction of robotics into restaurant kitchens may eventually reduce job opportunities for some culinary professionals. A company named Moley Robotics has created the world's first fully automated and intelligent cooking robot. The robot has two movable human-like arms that are installed above a specially built grill and food preparation area. According to Moley, "It can learn recipes, cook them, and clear up after itself!"

In the future, such robots will be integrated into the kitchens of large restaurants to perform basic food preparation and cooking tasks. But will robots eventually replace chefs? Perhaps so for food preparation workers, but probably not for chefs. We won't see robot chef kitchen armies for several reasons. Cooking is an art that requires a lot of creativity and knowledge of ingredients and cultures that no robot can completely master. Also, the upscale restaurant business is a personality-driven field. People often dine at popular restaurants because the food is wonderful and because of the reputation and celebrity of the chef. A popular chef brings people into a restaurant and makes its owners a lot of money. After the initial excitement of a robot cooking one's dinner, it's hard to see how people will get too excited about a robot chef. As a result, there will continue to be demand for chefs, especially at large restaurants.

IN CLOSING

Do you enjoy cooking and baking? Are you creative and like making other people happy? Do you have good leadership and people skills? If so, a career as a chef might be in your future. Use this book and other resources to continue to explore your interest in a career in the culinary arts. Do some more research. Visit culinary school websites. Read books about becoming a chef. Talk to any chefs you know, or find their contact information and email or call them. Most importantly, do some cooking to see if this career is a good fit for your skills and interests. Becoming a chef is hard work and takes many hours and a lot of dedication. But don't give up—you may find yourself making a great salary, meeting great people, and cooking great food. Good luck with your career exploration!

Working as a chef is a rewarding way to spend your life.

RESEARCH PROJECT

Talk to five chefs who work for different types of employers about the future of the career. Ask them how technology and other developments will change the field. Write a report that summarizes your findings and present it to your class.

TEXT-DEPENDENT QUESTIONS

1. Why is the employment outlook good for chefs?
2. What factors may cause employment for chefs to slow?
3. What is molecular gastronomy?

accreditation: The process of being evaluated and approved by a governing body as providing excellent coursework, products, or services. Quality college and university educational programs are accredited.

application materials: Items, such as a cover letter, resume, and letters of recommendation, that one provides to employers when applying for a job or an internship.

apprenticeship: A formal training program that combines classroom instruction and supervised practical experience. Apprentices are paid a salary that increases as they obtain experience.

associate's degree: A degree that requires a two-year course of study after high school.

bachelor's degree: A degree that requires a four-year course of study after high school.

certificate: A credential that shows a person has completed specialized education, passed a test, and met other requirements to qualify for work in a career or industry. College certificate programs typically last six months to a year.

certification: A credential that one earns by passing a test and meeting other requirements. Certified workers have a better chance of landing a job than those who are not certified. They also often earn higher salaries than those who are not certified.

community college: A private or public two-year college that awards certificates and associates degrees.

consultant: An experienced professional who is self-employed and provides expertise about a particular subject.

cover letter: A one-page letter in which a job seeker summarizes their educational and professional background, skills, and achievements, as well as states their interest in a job.

doctoral degree: A degree that is awarded to an individual who completes two or three additional years of education after earning a master's degree. It is also known as a **doctorate**.

for-profit business: One that seeks to earn money for its owners.

fringe benefits: A payment or non-financial benefit that is given to a worker in addition to salary. These consist of cash bonuses for good work, paid vacations and sick days, and health and life insurance.

information interview: The process of interviewing a person about their career, whether in person, by phone, online, or by email.

internship: A paid or unpaid learning opportunity in which a student works at a business to obtain experience for anywhere from a few weeks to a year.

job interview: A phone, internet, or in-person meeting in which a job applicant presents their credentials to a hiring manager.

job shadowing: The process of following a worker around while they do their job, with the goal of learning more about a particular career and building one's network.

licensing: Official permission that is granted by a government agency to a person in a particular field (nursing, engineering, etc.) to practice in their profession. Licensing requirements typically involve meeting educational and experience requirements, and sometimes passing a test.

master's degree: A two-year, graduate-level degree that is earned after a student first completes a four-year bachelor's degree.

mentor: An experienced professional who provides advice to a student or inexperienced worker (mentee) regarding personal and career development.

minimum wage: The minimum amount that a worker can be paid by law.

nonprofit organization: A group that uses any profits it generates to advance its stated goals (protecting the environment, helping the homeless, etc.). It is not a corporation or other for-profit business.

professional association: An organization that is founded by a group of people who have the same career (engineers, professional hackers, scientists, etc.) or who work in the same industry (information technology, health care, etc.).

professional network: Friends, family, coworkers, former teachers, and others who can help you find a job.

recruiting firm: A company that matches job seekers with job openings.

registered apprenticeship: A program that meets standards of fairness, safety, and training established by the U.S. government or local governments.

resume: A formal summary of one's educational and work experience that is submitted to a potential employer.

salary: Money one receives for doing work.

scholarship: Money that is awarded to students to pay for college and other types of education; it does not have to be paid back.

self-employed: Working for oneself as a small business owner, rather than for a corporation or other employer. Self-employed people must generate their own income and provide their own fringe benefits (such as health insurance).

soft skills: Personal abilities that people need to develop to be successful on the job—communication, work ethic, teamwork, decision-making, positivity, time management, flexibility, problem-solving, critical thinking, conflict resolution, and other skills and traits.

technical college: A public or private college that offers two- or four-year programs in practical subjects, such as the trades, information technology, applied sciences, agriculture, and engineering.

union: An organization that seeks to gain better wages, benefits, and working conditions for its members. Also called a **labor union** or **trade union**.

work-life balance: A healthy balance of time spent on the job and time spent with family and on leisure activities.

FURTHER READING

Beaupommier, Aurélia. *The Wizard's Cookbook: Magical Recipes Inspired by Harry Potter, Merlin, The Wizard of Oz, and More.* New York: Skyhorse Publishing, 2017.

Brown, Tracy. *Culinary Arts: A Practical Career Guide.* Lanham, MD: Rowman & Littlefield Publishers, 2019.

Donovan, Robin. *The Baking Cookbook for Teens: 75 Delicious Recipes for Sweet and Savory Treats.* Emeryville, CA: Rockridge Press, 2018.

Smith, Remmi. *The Healthy Teen Cookbook: Around the World in 80 Fantastic Recipes.* Miami: Mango, 2018.

INTERNET RESOURCES

www.bls.gov/ooh/food-preparation-and-serving/chefs-and-head-cooks.htm: This section of the *Occupational Outlook Handbook* features information on job duties, educational requirements, salaries, and the employment outlook for chefs and head cooks.

www.foodnetwork.com/profiles: Visit this website to read the biographies of well-known Food Network chefs such as Guy Fieri, Ina Garten, and Bobby Flay.

www.restaurant.org/Restaurant-Careers/Career-Development/Career-Options/Job-Titles: This website from the National Restaurant Association offers descriptions of more than twenty-five careers in the food service industry.

www.exploratorium.edu/cooking: Visit this website to learn more about the science behind cooking.

EDUCATIONAL VIDEO LINKS

Chapter 1

Learn what it takes to become a chef in a top-rated restaurant: http://x-qr.net/1JVy

Chapter 2

An award-winning chef provides advice to those who aspire to a career in the culinary arts: http://x-qr.net/1LYM

Chapter 5

Learn about the key skills for success for chefs: http://x-qr.net/1K5H

Chapter 5

The winner of a National SkillsUSA culinary competition discusses his love of the culinary arts and his training to become a chef: http://x-qr.net/1JFz

Chapter 6

Learn how robots may change the future of cooking: http://x-qr.net/1KEf

INDEX

Ramsay, Gordon, 47–48
Ray, Rachael, 12
recipes, 20–24, 32, 51–52, 56–57
research chef, 20
restaurant critic, 8
restaurant industry, 13
robotics, 69–70
rolling pin, 32

S
Sánchez, Aarón, 9–10
sauce, 32
sauté, 32
sauté chef, 20
scald, 32
Scheib, Walter, 19
seafood, 33
sear, 33
seasonings, 33
self-taught, 43–44, 56–57
sense of taste and smell, 52
Skills Compétences Canada, 59
SkillsUSA, 58–59
soufflé, 21, 33
sous chef, 18, 52
spatula, 33
spice, 33
stock, 33
summer camp, culinary, 61–62

T
tongs, 33
training for careers in food service, 35, 40–45, 55–62

V
vegan, 33
vegan chef, 13
vegetable chef, 20

W
whisk, 33

AUTHOR BIOGRAPHIES

Andrew Morkes has been a writer and editor for more than twenty-five years. He is the author of more than twenty-five books about college planning and careers, including all of the titles in this series, many titles in the Careers in the Building Trades series, the *Vault Career Guide to Social Media*, and *They Teach That in College!?: A Resource Guide to More Than 100 Interesting College Majors*, which was selected as one of the best books of the year by the library journal *Voice of Youth Advocates*. He is also the author and publisher of "The Morkes Report: College and Career Planning Trends" blog.

Christie Marlowe lives in Binghamton, New York, where she works as a writer and web designer. She has a degree in literature, cares strongly about the environment, and spends three or more nights a week wailing on her Telecaster.

PHOTO CREDITS

CHEF
A CULINARY ARTIST

CAREERS WITH EARNING POTENTIAL

CAR MECHANIC

CHEF

COSMETOLOGIST

DOG GROOMER

MASSAGE THERAPIST

FARMER

THE ARTS

PRESENTING
YOURSELF